HOW TO TALK TO STRANGERS

10 Proven Ways On How To Talk To Strangers Without Being Awkward: Perfect Your Social Skills, Master Small Talk, Make Real Friends And Communicate Effortlessly

BRIAN K. JOHNSON

Copyright © 2021

BRIAN K. JOHNSON

All right reserved

INTRODUCTION

I'm almost certain I am not by any means the only one who was more than once cautioned not to converse with outsiders. As children, we were trained that outsiders are terrible individuals and that we ought not to converse with them regardless.

Our Parents have reasons for not allowing us to speak with strangers. There are some mean and risky individuals out there, and as youngsters, we were not truly adept at knowing the aims of individuals we cooperated with. By revealing to us not to converse with outsiders, our folks were attempting to secure us.

As we develop into grown-ups, we figure out how to separate individuals with well-meaning goals from those with terrible expectations. We discover that most of individuals in the public arena are not sociopaths, that a great many people are entirely amicable. As a grown-up, it doesn't bode well to try not to converse with outsiders, in light of the fact that there isn't a lot to fear.

You can without much of a stretch tell whether an individual has vindictive goals and keep away from them. Notwithstanding, talking to strangers has great advantages. It assists us with extending our organization and assembles associations with others.

Sadly, in spite of having figured out how to tell great individuals from the individuals who mean us hurt, the dread of conversing with outsiders ingrained during our youth remains.

This is the reason a significant number of us feel uncomfortable with conversing with somebody we don't have the foggiest idea. The possibility of moving toward an outsider and starting a discussion makes us anxious. Along these lines, we close off ourselves in our own little world, inside our own little circles, and in this manner, we pass up freedoms to meet new, energizing individuals. As a grown-up, connecting with new individuals can possibly do you more great than hurt.

A few groups can start up a discussion with anybody even outsiders. If you have a social nervousness problem (Miserable), the prospect of conversing with an individual you don't know can be scary (especially when they are a position figure).

The best guidance for beginning a discussion is entirely basic—centre around the other individual or says something happy.

Your underlying objective is to offer an early expression, which doesn't need to be unpredictable. The purpose of saying that first is to allow you to say something different once the individual reacts.

Conversing with outsiders is nerve-wracking for a great many people, regardless of whether you're genuinely alluring and sure. However long the other individual is talking, you don't have to say anything past "mhmm," "disclose to me more," and "intriguing." That is far simpler than endeavouring to engage them with your own accounts.

Don't simply pose one inquiry and afterward proceed onward. When the other individual has completed their answer, ask a subsequent inquiry. This mitigates the danger you'll appear as though you're investigating or stalking them.

At the point when you first commence the discussion, you know for all intents and purposes nothing about this individual. That is the reason creator and speaker Brian k. Johnson proposes picking themes basic to both of you right now.

Your actual climate is consistently a sure thing. Search for something worth remarking on - the engineering, an intriguing piece of work of art, the tune that is playing, etc.

The other individual's attire can likewise fill in as an ice breaker, even though you need to try not to appear to be unpleasant. Offer commendations like, "Those shoes are quite one of a kind. Where did you get them?" and "I like your shirt's plan. Which brand is it?" instead of ones like, "Your shirt looks awesome."

Experts likewise suggest "responding to remarks in the soul they were given." When the other individual makes a joke, snicker - regardless of whether you didn't think it was a side-splitter. On the off chance that they offer an astonishing point of interest or tale - like "The absence of an Oxford comma could cost a Maine organization a large number of dollars in an additional time claim" - respond with shock. They'll feel satisfied by your reaction, which will make them need to continue to converse with you.

CHAPTER 1

Conversing With New Individuals

Why it is hard because there are such countless questions

Conversing with somebody you don't know is an unknown area. Contrasted with conversing with your accomplice, your dearest companion, or your mother, the questions make it trying and possibly scary.

You've most likely been advised not to converse with outsiders, but rather it tends to be truly remunerating to associate with individuals you don't have the foggiest idea. While it might appear to be a little extreme sorting out what to say, there are a ton of things you can do to make casual discussion with anybody that you meet. We'll begin with certain tips on amicable non-verbal communication and proceed onward to points you can raise to loosen things up and urge them to hold a discussion!

What does it take to say a straightforward hi to a more interesting you pass in the city? How should that collaboration proceed? What are the spots where you are bound to communicate with individuals you don't have the foggiest idea? How would you escape a discussion? These sound like simple inquiries. They are definitely not.

Think about the last discussion you had with somebody you didn't have a clue about. Did certain minutes feel abnormal? Did you track down the other individual intriguing? Did the other individual discover you intriguing? Is it safe to say that you were happy you had the discussion?

The other individual may go on and on. We may go on and on. They may close down. We may get exhausted. They may get exhausted. There may be an awkward quiet. They may be attempting to hit on me. They may be attempting to hurt me in one way or another. There are unwritten accepted practices in each unique circumstance, which we will in general need to follow, yet we may not generally make certain of. Will uncovering a specific reality about ourselves cause us to show up more trustworthy or amiable? Will being too intense dazzle or turn somebody off?

CHAPTER 2

We're Social Creatures

However, awkward communications sometimes are better for our progress.

Be that as it may, in spite of the uncomfortable silences, the slips up, and the uncertain balance, conversing with new individuals (even outsiders we probably will not see once more) is beneficial for us. Studies show that even negligible social associations (say, visiting with that stranger on the train) helps state of mind, for instance.

In one investigation, analysts selected people indiscriminately as they entered a packed café downtown Vancouver, guiding some to attempt to have a discussion with the barista and others to be just about as productive as conceivable in their espresso bringing. The previous gathering revealed leaving the bistro feeling better and having a superior feeling of having a place locally contrasted and the productive gathering.

CHAPTER 3

Below Are Ten Reasons Why You Ought To Start A Talk With Strangers.

1. It is a chance to make new companions

Companions are vital. Companions hold us back from being desolate, they urge us to pursue our fantasies, they show us new things, they help us settle on better decisions throughout everyday life; they help us manage pressure, and furnish us with help once we need it.

Different examinations have even shown that having a great deal of solid companionships is useful for your physical and psychological wellness.

However, here is the thing — you are not conceived along with your companions. In the event that you simply consider all of your dear companions today, they were all outsiders at one point throughout lifestyle.

Along these lines, on the off chance that you need to make more companions, you must converse with outsiders, who will at that point ideally transform into old buddies.

Every one of the outsiders you see around you consistently all current you with a chance to make another companion.

That person you chance upon at the exercise two or multiple times each week could be a possible work out accomplice.

The woman from the workplace close to yours?

Maybe she cherishes salsa however much you are doing and would adore somebody to travel together with her to manoeuvre classes.

Shockingly, you will not ever know whether you do not converse with them.

By keeping your mouth shut, you're denying yourself of the chance to satisfy an energizing individual and make another companion.

Along these lines, next time you chance upon that more odd you see consistently, go to them and initiate a discussion.

2. Outsiders could prompt new companions

While outsiders present freedoms for you to make new companions, you clearly will not get along with each new individual you converse with.

Be that as it may, you don't have the foggiest idea where the discussion may lead.

Regardless of whether you don't wind up making an association with the individual, they may acquaint you with another person who winds up turning into an old buddy.

For example, how about we expect that, in the wake of starting up a discussion with the woman from the workplace nearby, you discover that you don't actually share much for all intents and purpose.

Nonetheless, as you talk about your preferences and interests, she specifies that she has a companion who has an enthusiasm for exactly the same things as you.

Then again, the lady may welcome you to a gathering where you finish up gathering all the more new individuals and arising to be companions with a number of them.

3. Meet an expected mate

Conversing with outsiders likewise gives you a chance to meet the adoration for your life.

Consider your present heartfelt accomplice or somebody you at any point dated previously.

For the greater part of you, this individual was before a more interesting who later transformed into a darling. I'm living evidence of this.

There is this one time I went to an eatery, and since it was very full, I needed to impart a table to a lovely woman.

I said howdy to her and we occupied with some casual discussion as we hung tight for our dinners.

We ended up exchanging phone numbers.

This prompted more discussions and more snacks together.

At last, the more peculiar I chose to converse with at the eatery wound up turning into my awesome spouse.

Actually like for my situation, conversing with outsiders furnishes you with a chance to meet an expected mate.

That man or woman sitting on the brink of you on the train or remaining on the road with you at the overall store might be your perfect partner.

Nonetheless, you won't ever know whether you don't converse with them.

Best of all, you do not need to utilize any messy pickup lines or another such stuff.

Essentially be well disposed, start up an easy-going discussion and see where it leads.

4. Gain another viewpoint

In some cases, conversing with outsiders doesn't prompt companionships or new heartfelt connections. Quite possibly you will entirely meet a portion of these individuals once more.

In any case, having even that one discussion with them can be a stunner.

The outsider may change your viewpoint and give you another perspective on that you have never thought of.

5. Extend your business organization

In your expert life, your organization is vital.

Your organization opens up promising circumstances for new business and new openings, assists you with ascending the professional bureaucracy, grows your encouraging group of people, makes you more noticeable, assists you with studying your field, etc.

This is the reason essentially all vocation mentors laud the significance of systems administration.

Here is that the kicker – organizing expects you to effectively leave and converse with outsiders.

Systems administration occasions are basically stages for outsiders with normal interests to meet and converse with one another.

On the off chance that the solitary individuals you at any point converse with are your family members and dear companions, you can disregard fabricating a business organization.

Numerous fruitful individuals really admit that the best breaks and openings in their expert lives came due to conversing with outsiders.

Along these lines, in your expert life, you should make it a propensity to converse with outsiders consistently.

As these individuals abandon outsiders into colleagues and presumably companions, no one can really tell which one of them will give you a chance that will help advance your vocation.

6.Conversing with outsiders could prompt extraordinary fun

Conversing with outsiders can likewise be extraordinary fun and compensate for an unconstrained, energizing day.

In reality, for certain individuals, the delight of voyaging comes from meeting outsiders and having encounters they had not made arrangements for. I can review a few occasions in my day to day existence where conversing with an outsider wound up making for an unconstrained and thrilling experience.

There is this one time I was holiday on Lamu Island.

While eating at my lodging, I got into a discussion with some person, and he welcomed me to a gathering that was he was going to.

I chose to follow along for the gathering, which was being hung on a gliding bar smack in the centre of the sea.

That gathering ended up being perhaps the best second I had during my excursion, and this happened in light of the fact that I coincidentally talked to an outsider at the inn.

Actually like my experience during my excursion, starting up discussions with outsiders can zest up your experience and lead to loads of fun.

7. You never know you may meet – it's your opportunity to discover

The most awesome aspect of conversing with outsiders is that no one can tell who you may meet.

The individual running on the treadmill on the brink of you'll have an open position for you, they'll get on the lookout for the piece of land you're attempting to sell, they may run for president one day (who wouldn't adore being a dear companion to the president), or they may end turning into your significant other or spouse.

You have in a real sense no clue about what's in store from the communication except if you really venture up and start a discussion with the outsider.

By conversing with them, you open up a universe of varied prospects. You don't have the foggiest idea what openings you miss by minding your own business.

8. Improve your social abilities

On the off chance that you need to accomplish a lot, both in your expert and individual life, you need to realize how to impart and connect with others.

Numerous fruitful individuals will reveal to you that a lot of their prosperity can be ascribed to their brilliant relationship building abilities.

Your social abilities are very much like some other expertise – they improve the more you practice, and you get corroded the more you abandon rehearsing them.

Conversing with outsiders consistently gives you the ideal chance to rehearse and improve this significant expertise.

As you converse with individuals you have never conversed with, the more you figure out how to make casual discussion, how to begin discussions, how to split away from discussions, and how to by and large have drawing in and significant collaborations with others.

9. Learn new things

As the regular saying goes, people with similarities tend to group together. The majority of your dear companions are very much like you.

They presumably like exactly the same things as you, they have comparative instructive achievements, they make practically a similar measure of cash as you, you know practically comparable things, you have comparative perspectives, etc.

Cooperating with this nearby circles and associates constantly restricts your capacity to learn new things.

Outsiders, then again, are nothing similar to you.

They don't have similar encounters as you, their instructive accomplishments are not the same as yours, their perspective is unique, their inclinations are extraordinary, etc.

Conversing with outsiders, consequently, gives you a chance to learn new things that you wouldn't gain from your group of friends.

10. Lift your certainty

The greater part of us feels restless at whatever point we consider drawing nearer and conversing with outsiders.

We begin questioning ourselves and think about every one of the things that could turn out badly.

Be that as it may, there is something I discover astonishing about nervousness.

The more you do things that make you anxious, the less apprehensive you feel, and the more sure you become.

By making it a propensity to converse with a few outsiders consistently, you step by step begin getting more alright with starting discussions with outsiders, and your self-assurance goes up.

At whatever point you end up in friendly circumstances, you quit feeling abnormal or bashful in light of the fact that you are now used to cooperating with outsiders.

This likewise gives you the certainty to acquaint yourself with individuals you need to meet for reasons unknown (like an expected boss or a possible date).

CHAPTER 4

Comprehensive Ways On How To Talk Better To A Stranger

1. Find somebody who looks open to discussion.

Watch the individual's non-verbal communication to check whether they're agreeable and open. Prior to moving toward an alien to talk, hold back to check whether they're grinning or visually connecting with individuals. In the event that they're now having a discussion with somebody, check on the off chance that they're utilizing hand motions and listening when the other individual talks. In the event that they look open to mingling, they're likely truly simple to converse with and will not care either way if you attempt to have a discussion with them.

•If somebody has their arms crossed or is staying away from others, they may not be in the temperament to converse with anybody.

•Only approach an outsider on the off chance that you have a sense of security around them. In the event that you feel awkward or at serious risk, pay attention to your gut feelings and stay away from the individual.

2. *Visually connect and grin.*

Indeed, even an amicable articulation can help you sense that you're mingling. Individuals are bound to start up a discussion in the event that they have a feeling that they can confide in you. Momentarily look toward them and attempt to bolt eyes regardless of whether it's only briefly. It's totally typical to feel somewhat scared, yet attempt to present a comforting grin and perceive how the other individual reacts. In the event that they grin back, it's a decent sign that they're willing to stop and visit for a brief period.

•Smiling likewise establishes an uplifting vibe and helps keep the discussion light and glad.

3. *Utilize open and connecting with non-verbal communication.*

Change your stance to appear to be more receptive. Keep your arms uncrossed so you look open and open to conversing with somebody. Turn your body towards the individual you need to converse with and slender somewhat toward them to show that you're keen on visiting. In the event that it assists you with feeling greater, envision the individual as an old buddy so you're considerably more loose around them.

•Practice your non-verbal communication before a mirror to perceive what transforms you need to make.

4. Regard their own space.

Getting excessively close may cause the individual to feel awkward. Everyone has diverse actual limits, so ensure you don't meddle with them. Focus on the individual's non-verbal communication to check whether they're getting some distance from you or looking away regularly, which may be signs that they're apprehensive. In the event that they seem as though they're uncomfortable, make a stride back from them and be respectful about how they respond.

•Other individuals may be apprehensive or scared to converse with you as well. By showing that you're cordial, you can help the other individual feel more loose.

•Respecting individual space is a two-way road, so make certain to shout out on the off chance that somebody causes you to feel awkward also. For instance, in the event that somebody goes in for an embrace, you can say, "God help us thank you, I'm not a major hugger."

5. Make proper acquaintance.

Beginning with a speedy hello could start a full discussion. As you're strolling through a gathering of individuals, attempt to say something brief to everybody you run into. We that it tends to be somewhat unnerving, however you could attempt "Hey," "Hi," or "Ideal to meet you" to loosen things up and show that you're willing to visit with them. Regardless of whether you don't possess a ton of energy for a meaningful discussion, welcoming the individual is as yet a pleasant signal that makes you all the more amicable.

•While it may make a few group awkward, others may welcome you back and need to proceed with the discussion.

•If welcoming individuals alone causes you to feel anxious, ask a companion or somebody you know to go with you.

6. Present yourself.

Loosen things up with a fast and well-disposed introduction. Since you don't have the foggiest idea about the individual, you don't need to give them your whole foundation. Try not to be hesitant to give them as much close-to-home data as you feel well with, regardless of whether it's simply your first name. In case you're in a business setting, you can likewise make reference to your work title if it's pertinent to the discussion.

•For model, you could say, "Hello, I'm Brad. I work at XYZ Distributing."

•Keep the group environment as a primary concern when you welcome somebody. For instance, on the off chance that you meet somebody at a parent's occasion at school, you could say, "Hi, I'm Janice. I have a girl in 3rd grade."

•You can generally uncover more data about yourself on the off chance that you wind up getting into a more profound conversation with the individual.

7. Learn and utilize their name.

Drop their name in the discussion to build up a superior association. Individuals appreciate hearing the sound of their own name, so make certain to ask the individual for theirs immediately. At the point when it feels normal to do it, say their name a couple of times while you're talking. The individual will feel like they're really holding with you and will urge them to be amicable back.

•Mentioning their name a couple of times likewise assists you with recollecting that it better so you're more averse to fail to remember it on the off chance that you chance upon one another once more.

8. Notice something in your environmental factors.

Pick something fascinating close by to use as a bouncing off point. In the event that you don't have a clue about the individual by any means, check out the room and raise something you see. You've most likely begun casual conversation about the climate; however you could likewise discuss the host of the gathering, the food, or others at the occasion. In case you're simply conversing with somebody you chanced upon, you could specify a close by store or the traffic.

•For model, in case you're beginning a discussion with somebody holding on to go across the road, you could say, "The traffic is insane today. Have you at any point seen it get this occupied?"

•As another model, in case you're at the supermarket, you could ask, "Have you attempted this brand of pasta sauce previously? It sounds great yet I've never had it."

9. Raise general subjects.

Strike up some casual conversation over mainstream society or recent developments. Generally, referencing on-going news or an encounter you've shared is an extraordinary beginning stage in case you're outsiders. Try not to stress in case you're somewhat scared; you can raise simple subjects like a Program or film you've seen, a book you've perused, or an image you saw on the web. On the off chance that you feel somewhat more alright with the individual, you can have a go at trying things out by raising family, work, and dating to check whether they need to open up additional.

•As another model, you could say, "Did you get the new scene of Risk? They had some truly intense inquiries this time around."

•If the individual doesn't appear to be keen on a theme, change the subject.

10. Praise them.

A commendation is a characteristic and complimenting approach to loosen things up. Notice something explicitly that you appreciate or like about them so you sound genuine. You could remark on something the individual's wearing, how they handle a circumstance, or whatever else you respect. After you loosen things up, keep visiting so you can study the individual.

•For model, you could say something like, "I love those shoes! Where did you get them?" or "That shirt tone truly flies on you!"

•As another model, you could say, "You truly took care of that contention with a ton of effortlessness."

•Avoid remarking on somebody's actual appearance a lot since it could make a few group awkward.

11. Ask them open-finished inquiries.

Discover more about the other individual so you can become acquainted with them better. Individuals love to discuss themselves, so get some information about, what they need to do throughout everyday life, and what encounters they've had. Attempt to pose open-finished inquiries that the individual needs to reply in more detail to make a big difference for the discussion. Some great icebreaker addresses you can ask include:

•What do you get a kick out of the chance to get done for entertainment only?

•What's the best thing that is happened to you this year?

•What would you say you are anticipating?

•How do you know the host of this gathering?

12. Offer things about yourself.

Opening up urges the other individual to begin talking as well. On the off chance that the individual doesn't offer a great deal toward the beginning of the discussion, accept the open door to go into things about your life or interests. You could specify your work, leisure activities, projects that you've done, or about how you know the host at a gathering. As you talk more, the other individual may feel greater discussing themselves to you.

•It's OK to keep a portion of your own subtleties hidden. Just raise the points that you feel good sharing.

13. Examine basic interests.

Track down some shared belief to carry on the discussion. In the event that the individual livens up when you notice your number one pastime, sports group, or something else you like, dive into the theme significantly more. Discussion regarding why you love it and ask the other individual for their sentiments also. Try not to pass judgment or scrutinize them in the event that they have an alternate assessment on it, yet be open and responsive to what in particular they're discussing.

•For model, you could say, "I saw you're wearing a Packers shirt and I love them. Did you get the game a weekend ago?"

•As another model, you could say, "Gracious, I truly like scuba plunging as well! What are your number one jumping spots?"

14. Listen effectively.

Stay drew in with the individual so they feel heard. As the other individual is talking, visually connect with them and gesture alongside the thing they're saying. Abstain from checking your telephone or getting occupied by different things so you don't lose centre. Offers up some short assertions, for example, "mmhmm" or "no doubt" to show that you're following the discussion.

•Be aware of your looks and be mindful so as not to scowl or give indications of revulsion since that can kill the other individual.

15. End the discussion following 5–10 minutes.

Watch for signals that the other individual needs to end the discussion. An easy-going discussion normally just a brief time before somebody needs to proceed onward. In the event that you've effectively talked for 5–10 minutes, the other individual should proceed onward. Something else, check in the event that they're getting more nervous, checking their telephone, or checking the time. Tell them that it was decent conversing with them and say you need to get moving. On the off chance that you delighted in the discussion, inquire as to whether they need to keep in contact later.

•For model, you could say, "I had a truly happy time visiting with you. Would you like to trade numbers and talk again later?"

CHAPTER 5

A Definitive Manual For Small Talks: Ice Breakers, Amazing Inquiries, And More

Like it or not, casual chitchat is fundamental to your prosperity.

Regardless of whether you're organizing, talking with another possibility, or heating up a client prior to upselling them, or requesting a reference, you should have the option to fabricate affinity with easy-going discussion.

To help you ace this vital ability, we've composed an exhaustive manual for casual banter.

What Is Small Talk

Small Talk/Casual chitchat is a light, casual discussion. It's ordinarily utilized when you're conversing with somebody you don't know quite well and at systems administration and get-togethers.

The most effective method to Make Casual chitchat

There are four techniques that will help you make casual discussion in any circumstance.

First, pose open-finished inquiries.

The vast majority appreciate discussing themselves - not exclusively are we are our number one subjects, but on the other hand it's simpler to examine yourself than something you think minimal about. Consider the big picture: Would you make some harder memories talking about fourteenth century glass-blowing or your #1 book? Open-finished inquiries create an intriguing, unique discussion and support the individual you're talking with to open up.

Second, practice undivided attention.

It's enticing to block out at times, however you'll fashion a lot more grounded associations on the off chance that you focus. The other individual will see how drawn in you appear. Likewise, it's a lot simpler to pose applicable inquiries and recall subtleties to raise later in case you're not tuning in with one ear.

Third, set aside your telephone.

We will in general draw out our telephones when we're feeling awkward or abnormal in friendly circumstances, yet nothing will disrupt your conversational endeavours all the more rapidly. Barely any individuals will move toward you in case you're looking through your telephone - and you'll send a plain message to anybody you're now conversing with that you're not intrigued.

Fourth, show your excitement.

Casual conversation may not generally be the most peaceful movement. Notwithstanding, in the event that you go into it with the correct mentality, you can really have a great time. View these discussions as freedoms to study others. No one can tell whom you'll meet or what they'll need to share - so embrace the opportunity it'll be an astounding conversation.

CHAPTER 6

Casual Chitchat/Small Talk Subjects

- Your area or scene
- Shows, films, play, and so on
- Art
- Food, eateries, or cooking
- Their pastimes
- Their expert interests and obligations
- Sports
- The environment
- Travel
- Their nearby top choices

Having great casual discussion subjects at your disposal will not simply help you kick off incredible discussions, it'll likewise ease a portion of the tension of strolling into an obscure climate.

1. The area or the scene

Talk about your environmental factors. Is it true that you are in a delightful lodging, home, or gathering territory? Is the town critical? Did you as of late visit some place cool close by?

2. Amusement

Discussion about what you've delighted in of late and what's on your rundown. That may incorporate the Netflix show both of you are marathon watching, the last film every one of you saw, the books you're perusing, the webcasts you're streaming, any plays you've joined in, etc.

3. Craftsmanship

In the event that the individual you're addressing appreciates workmanship, ask them which historical centres they've gone to and might want to visit, their number one shows, which specialists they appreciate, in the event that they have any proposals for displays, which kind and vehicle of craftsmanship they like, how their advantage created, etc.

You can likewise talk about changes in the craftsmanship world. Are there any recent fads creating they're keen on (like "post-web craftsmanship")? What are their considerations?

4. Food

Food is a standout amongst other casual chitchat subjects, since nearly everybody loves to eat. Ask which eateries they'd suggest and the dishes you should arrange. On the off chance that they don't eat out frequently, ask which dishes they like to make at home. Depict an impending situation and hear their point of view on what you should cook or bring. For instance, "I'm answerable for dessert for a housewarming party. There are 10 individuals coming - two vegetarians, one individual with a nut hypersensitivity, and another who doesn't eat gluten. What might you recommend?"

5. Leisure activities

Dive into the other individual's interests. They'll be energetic to discuss what they love, and you'll find the opportunity to interface with them on a more profound level.

Ask what they do in their extra energy, which exercises they partake in outside of work (and how they got included), what their youth side interests were versus now, regardless of whether they're taking any classes, and what they'd prefer to attempt (sushi-production, novel-composing, salsa moving, and so forth)

6. Work

Discussing your day occupations can be precarious. You don't need the discussion to regress into an exhausting correlation of what you do - which it rapidly will except if you steer toward a seriously fascinating area.

Then again, work is a decent casual conversation point on the grounds that by far most of the individuals have a comment.

Rather than posing conventional inquiries like, "Where accomplish your work?" "How long have you worked there?" and "Do you like it?" utilize fascinating, startling ones, for example,

•"My [niece/child/grandchild] needs to turn into a [profession]. Do you have any guidance I should pass on?"

•"What's your number one part of your work? For what reason did you choose to work in [A particular job]?"

•"Many of my clients in [A particular role] disclose to me [things about occupation]. Has that remained constant as far as you can tell?"

•"What are your major role at work? Is that what you anticipated?"

•"What's the generalization of a [job title]? Does it hold up?"

•"Let me know if there is anything you don't like about this job? Do you like or aversion that?"

7. Sports

A few groups could discuss sports the entire day. Others would prefer to discuss anything other than. There are a couple of general guidelines for examining sports.

In the first place, in case you're in a gathering of two or more individuals, ensure everybody is an avid supporter. You would prefer not to reject somebody from taking an interest. Second, while an eager discussion is fun, a warmed one will not assistance your systems administration objectives at all. On the off chance that you or the other individual beginnings getting disturbed up, change the subject.

8. The climate

Climate is a definitive casual chitchat subject. It's regularly not the most glimmering ice breaker, but rather with a little inventiveness you can start some captivating conversations.

Get some information about the other individual's arrangements given the climate (for instance, if it's stormy would they say they will remain at home and watch motion pictures? In the event that it's bright, would they say they will have a barbeque, accomplish something outdoorsy, go on a climb, have supper on their porch, and so on?)

You can likewise examine their #1 kind of environment and why they like it. This habitually transforms into a conversation about their character, which can be fun and intriguing.

Make them talk about the environment in their old neighbourhood. Is it not the same as where they reside now? The equivalent? Which type do they appreciate more? In the event that they could decide to live anyplace dependent on the climate conditions, where might it be?

Occasional customs and customs are convenient ice breakers also. Do they do anything unique this season? Are there any spots they visit, trips they take, individuals they see, or different exercises they do?

9. Travel

Not every person you talk with will be a world explorer; however inquiring as to whether they've voyaged anyplace intriguing of late can open up a universe of conceivable outcomes. From weekend trips an hour away to enormous summer excursions, or list of must-dos ventures - this inquiry can get even the most saved possibilities spouting about valued recollections or energizing forthcoming undertakings.

Ensure you have some subsequent inquiries concerning what they intend to do on their excursion. What food sources they're generally eager to attempt. Also, what trinkets they want to get back.

10. Their neighbourhood top picks

A researcher has a stunt each rep can utilize. Prior to a call with a possibility, he Google's their town. Frequently, individuals he's talking with life in towns He rarely visited, however with a two-minute pursuit, he thinks about their most sizzling new eatery, what the climate resembles right now, and which tourist spots local people love.

He utilizes this information to wow his possibilities with questions like, "Have you made it to [Insert up and coming neighbourhood play here] yet?" or "Would you say you are remaining cool over yonder? I hear it will be during the '90s this week." This additional progression reassures the possibility, shows them Dan thinks often about what they care about and assembles quick affinity.

CHAPTER 7

Ice Breakers

For possibilities:

•"What's the most energizing thing about your business?"

•"What's the most energizing thing about your item?"

•"What's the most energizing thing about your group?"

•"What's the most energizing thing about your industry?"

•"I'm inquisitive to know your story."

•"Tell me about your features at [company name]."

•"Tell me about your lowlights at [company name]."

•"What's your greatest need at the present time?"

•"What's your most reduced need?"

•"What is your manager focused on this moment?"

•"What's your main most significant measurement?"

For clients:

•"How are things going?"

•"What's your advancement on a particular area?"

•"What would you say you are stressed over?"

•"What would you say you are glad about?"

•"How are your endeavours in [related business area]?"

•"How's life?"

For proficient colleagues:

•"What's your industry like at the present time?"

•"Do you need any presentations?"

•"Tell me about your most recent work win."

The ideas above are extraordinary umbrella themes for casual banter, yet you may be searching for explicit inquiries.

Here are not many that have demonstrated to function admirably.

CHAPTER 8

Casual Conversation Questions

1."How was [happenings]? In case you could snap your fingers to in a brief instant bring your [co-trained professional, boss, best friend], all right? Why or why not?"

2."What's been the work schedule of your [day, week, and month] up until this moment?"

3."Are you a long way from home?"

4."Would you allow us to have that [Something they're holding]?"

5."Tell me about the last? How did it go?"

6."What work ethics do you prefer?"

CHAPTER 9

Best Strategy To End A Conversation

It's in a like manner helpful to have a setup exit. If the conversation is easing back down - or it's basically finished and you need a non-messed up way to deal with leave - use this line to easily wrap things up.

Here are 5 potential leave lines:

1."This has been phenomenal -Nice for teaching me in regards to X. Do you have a card?"

2."Let me get [clothes]. Uncommon to [meet you, get up]."

3."We are starting soon, so I need to prepare."

4."Excuse me, I will use the restroom. Like the rest of the [event, party, conference]."

5."Well, glad we discovered the chance to interface over [topic]. I would not really like to overpower your [morning, evening, night] - I'm going to [check out the goodies, make appropriate colleague with someone, take a walk around the setting, etc.]"

CHAPTER 10

Guidelines To Improve At Casual Chitchat Conversation

It doesn't have any effect on how terrible you are at easy-going conversation: With preparing and the right situation, you can improve. The easy-going conversation is an aptitude really like some other.

Quest for opportunities to make easy-going discussion.

The more as regularly as conceivable you do it, the more pleasing you'll transform into. You'll moreover quickly acknowledge which subjects make the best conversations, how to gauge a person's attitude and character by their non-verbal correspondence and way of talking when to change the subject matter, and this shows that the communication has ended.

To diminish your misgiving, practice your easy-going conversation in a low-stakes environment. Go to a nice frameworks organization event for a substitute industry; go to a social gathering or solicitation that your partners bring you along to their work events.

You can in like manner "train" by speaking with outcasts when you're all over town - basically guarantee you don't oblige a conversation with any person who's unquestionably not captivated.

2. Envision you're tending to a partner.

Would you be restless if you were making easy-going discussions with someone you knew really well? Apparently not. If you need a quick trick to calm your anxiety, envision the other individual as an old mate. As an extra benefit, this mental shift will make you seem, by all accounts, to be sultrier and more neighbourly.

3. Offer yourself relief.

Do whatever it takes not to nag messed up minutes or long calms. We're all certainly more revolved around and censuring of ourselves than some other individual in the room. You might be withdrawing for a seriously long time after you mix up someone's name or tell a joke that fails spectacularly, anyway chances are, every single other indIvidual will forget inside two minutes.

At whatever point you're worried about a specific socially abnormal demonstration, remind yourself its way off the mark as huge a plan as you would speculate.

4. Set a target.

Having an objective can make easy-going talk feel more critical. For example, maybe you centre around get-together four people at an event or exchanging contact information with two unique specialists in your field.

At whatever point you have a strong target, you'll feel deliberate and trotted. This also allows you to fair measure your thriving.

CHAPTER 11

Staying Away From Small Talk / Conversation

It may appear senseless to compose an all-inclusive post about casual banter - and afterward dig into strategies for staying away from it.

In any case, let's get straight to the point. This isn't a manual for avoiding discussions at systems administration occasions, office gatherings, meetings, or get-togethers. In the event that you need to do that, I have a straightforward idea: Remain at home!

Obviously, that is typically not a possible technique on the off chance that you need to fashion new associations (and since producing new associations will in general go inseparably with vocation development, I energetically suggest doing it incidentally).

Staying away from casual chitchat = abstaining from exhausting, prosaic, trivial, forgettable discussions that don't enhance you or different members.

In the event that you need to do that, here are a couple of ideas. (Incidentally, keeping away from casual banter is one of my constant objectives throughout everyday life.)

To start with, be interested. The individual or individuals you're conversing with are fascinating. Odds are, they know a ton about something you know something about - if very few things. Exploit that. Sort out what they care about and pose loads of inquiries. Remember to tune in and stay connected so it's unmistakable you're not simply making a cursory effort.

Second, suggest interesting conversation starters and start non-clear conversations. In the event that you say something like, "It's so chilly this week," you will have a meh discussion (except if you're conversing with a rancher or meteorologist, possibly). Get inventive and possibly somewhat strange. At the point when somebody says, "Goodness, it's so chilly this week," answer, "Sure is. Did you experience childhood in a hotter region?" Presently you're discussing their adolescence and the better places they've lived. Way seriously intriguing.

Third, keep away from super questionable or delicate subjects. These include:

1. Politics

2. Physical appearance

3. Religion

4. Age

5. Anything PG-13 and up

CONCLUSION

Regardless of whether your mom instructed you to take a gander at outsiders with doubt, the vast majority out there are not hoping to grab you or loot you. They are essentially individuals, very much like you.

Keep in mind, every one of your companions began as outsiders, and there is no motivation behind why you ought not to transform more outsiders into companions and associates.

Contacting outsiders and making associations with them furnishes you with freedoms to make new companions and perhaps even meet your perfect partner, acquire new viewpoint, grow your organization, learn new things, improve your social abilities and confident have some good times encounters.

Having taken in the advantages of conversing with outsiders and tips on the best way to really converse with outsiders, I ask you to make a propensity for conversing with in any event two new individuals every day.

Regardless of whether you love making casual discussion or wish you never needed to do it, these tips, ice breakers, and questions will assist you with taking full advantage of it. I wish you Best of luck out there.

www.ingramcontent.com/pod-product-compliance
Lightning Source LLC
Chambersburg PA
CBHW061717130726
47996CB00006B/2366